Wedding

Budget

Hacks

Discover The Secrets The Industry Doesn't

Want You To Know About Planning Your

Dream Wedding Under Budget & Without

Compromise

Aliesha Garrod

Contents

Acknowledgements

There are several people and parties without whom this book could have never become a reality.

I would like to extend my thanks to:

My cousin Jaimie Morton-McCourt of MC C Photography for the photograph of me used on the rear cover.

With very special thanks to my Husband, Josh Garrod, for your dedicated support and assistance with the authoring and publishing of this book. I would not have come this far without your motivation and encouragement.

To my children, Caleb & Lincoln, who inspire me every day to do more and be better.

To my parents, Lyn and Steve for your continued support in everything I do.

And to the rest of my family and friends for being there with me every step of the way, throughout my journey.

Introduction

My name is Aliesha Garrod. I help busy women who are planning weddings make the very best of their two most important assets: time and money.

In August 2017, my husband and I got married. It was everything we wanted and more. We had a £30,000 wedding for a little under £15,000! We were also able to achieve this with absolutely **no debt** whatsoever.

In this book, you will discover the closely guarded secrets that the Wedding Industry doesn't want you to know that will help *you* plan a wedding **under budget** without compromising on what you want.

These are the exact tactics and strategies that my husband and I used that enabled us to save a massive 50% off of the cost our wedding.

When asked, "Budget" is one of the most common things that Will-Be-Brides struggle with. Questions and problems surrounding budgets could cover all sorts of different areas. I wanted to find out exactly what future brides were struggling with as far as the Wedding Budget was concerned.

So, I dug a little deeper and found out that ladies planning their weddings were struggling with just about every aspect of the budget, ranging from the actual funding of the wedding itself, to deciding how much should be allocated to each individual piece of it.

I wrote this book to share with you some facts, my thoughts, feelings and ideas to help you overcome any Wedding Budget issues you might currently be suffering with.

This book has been designed as a practical workbook that will take you on a journey, and hopefully clear up most, if not all, of your Wedding Budget concerns.

Chapter One -
Budget Discovery

How Long Until "The Big Day"?

One of the very first questions you need to answer before you even think about setting a budget for your wedding is "How long do we have until The Big Day?" - that is, assuming you have already decided on a date to Tie The Knot.

If you're still to book a venue, you should think carefully about *when* you should plan your wedding for a very good reason: the amount of time you have from now until the Wedding will likely have an impact on the amount of funds you will have access to for spending on your wedding, also known as your "Budget".

Of course, there will be those of you who are the exceptions to the rule and have been planning your weddings for the last ten years and saving along the way (I was planning mine for years on Pinterest before I was even engaged - I just forgot to save). If that's you, well done! You're ahead of the game and will likely have a more substantial budget to work with. For the rest of us, however, things can be a little more challenging.

The average Bride-to-Be spends a total of twelve months planning her Wedding, from the point of getting Engaged to actually Tying The Knot. This is not a huge amount of time in the scheme of things, when you think about what needs to be done in that time!

Chances are, the proposal came out of the blue. And while you want to be able to have the wedding of your dreams, I know you're keen to get hitched as soon as you possibly can. So, if you set yourselves a budget of £25,000 for your wedding, is saving that kind of cash achievable in that period of time?

Who's Paying For What?

The fact is, every one of you will be in a different situation financially. So, it's important to look at who is going to be paying for your wedding; some of you might have loved ones willing to contribute, while others may not.

According to a recent survey by hitched.co.uk:

- 36% of couples fund their own wedding

- 48% of couples had the assistance of both families

- 5% of couples had the Bride's family cough up

Safe to say that the old "tradition" of the Bride's parents paying for the wedding has died off significantly in the 21st Century. It is easy to see why too. We've been living with our parents for a lot longer than our parents lived with theirs.

The same survey conducted by hitched.co.uk shows that the average age of a Bride is 33 and for a Groom 34. This is quite a change from what was considered "the norm" just 25 years ago. My own parents were married and moved out by the ages of 21 (Mum) and 24 (Dad)

Also, many of us are waiting longer to get married these days too. The stigma that used to be attached to living as a couple and having children together before marriage is almost non-existent today.

Taking this data into account throughout the remainder of this book, I am going to assume that you plan on funding at least part of, if not all, of your wedding yourself.

Having the conversation with your respective families about paying for the Wedding can be extremely uncomfortable, and in my opinion, should be avoided at all costs. Once you announce your engagement to the world, anyone who has any intention of assisting you with the cost of your Wedding will usually make themselves known at this point. If they don't immediately offer any financial support, but they surprise you later on down the line and offer to help with the costs, then it will be a bonus and help you to stay under budget.

I have discovered an alternative approach to simply asking for a lump of money, and that is to present your budget list (which we will be creating later on in this book), detailing all of the estimated expenditure, to any willing contributors. The contributors can then decide which part of the wedding they would like to support you with.

I have spoken to many Brides who felt a sort of obligation to compromise on their wants for their own weddings in order to accommodate the preferences of those contributing, and later regretted it. Please **do not** fall into this trap. It is easy to do since it would usually be considered rude to ignore other people's wishes. However, *your* Wedding Day is an exception to this unwritten rule. There are ways to politely communicate this to a persistent contributor who has other ideas about your Wedding. These can be found in your Member's Area for Busy Bride Club.

Side Note: *If you're not already a member of Busy Bride Club, you can sign up at BusyBrideClub.com - you'll get our Ultimate Wedding Planning Pack FREE when you join.*

Your Monthly Available Money

This seems like a fairly obvious thing to consider when setting your budget, but you would not believe how many Brides-to-Be set their budget without giving any thought to their income.

Let's kick things off with a little exercise that will help move us a step closer to setting your budget.

First, start by writing yours and your partner's **take home** monthly income. This amount should be after any tax and National Insurance so we know exactly what you have coming into your household. Your take home income added to your partner's take home income gives you your **Total Monthly Household Income**.

Tip: *These exercises are best done with your partner.*

Your Take Home Income p/m	
Your Partner's Take Home Income p/m	
Total Monthly Household Income:	

Now that we know how much money you have coming in each month, we need to figure out how much is actually left over once you've paid your bills and other required financial commitments.

Fill in the table below as accurately as you can and try not to forget anything. This should once again be on a monthly basis. Add the subtotal from your **Standard Household Expenses** to the subtotal from the additional lifestyle expenses to give you your **Total Monthly Expenditure**.

This is going to require you to be brutally honest with yourself about your expenses, including those takeaways you have and maybe that Costa on the way to work every day.

TIP: When I did this exercise myself, I found it really useful to have my Internet Banking open on my laptop and to look through all of my Direct Debit and Standing Order commitments, then look through the past 6 months of statements to find any other consistent costs that I had (i.e. fuel for the car, groceries, etc).

Standard Household Expenses	
Mortgage / Rent	
Council Tax	
Home Insurance	
Heating, Power & Water	
Home Phone & Broadband	
TV Licence & Subscriptions (inc. streaming services)	

Car Insurance & Tax	
Fuel for the Car(s)	
Groceries	
Mobile Phone Contracts	
Finance / Loan Payments	
Credit Card Payments	
Child Care, Nursery & Pre-School	
Commuting Expenses (train, bus, etc)	
Health (prescriptions, dentist, etc)	
Pets (pet insurance, vet bills, etc)	
General Household Expenses (window cleaner, maintenance, etc)	
Child Maintenance (commitments from previous relationships, if any)	
Subtotal:	

Additional Lifestyle Expenses	
Entertainment (eating out, cinema, etc)	
Takeaways	
Luxury Items (clothes, makeup, etc)	
Gift Expenditure (Birthdays, Christmas, etc)	
Gym Membership	
Habits (smoking, drinking, etc)	
Holidays & Short Breaks	
Other miscellaneous	
Subtotal:	
Total Monthly Expenditure:	

Your **Total Monthly Expenditure** should be less than your **Total Monthly Household Income**. If not, you've likely got your numbers wrong somewhere.

We need to do another little sum to arrive at what I call your "**Monthly Disposable Income**". This is the money that is left over once everything else has been paid for.

The equation looks like this:

Total Monthly Household Income - Total Monthly Expenditure

= Monthly Disposable Income

Monthly Disposable Income	

If nothing were to change, your **Monthly Disposable Income** is what you have to save each month for your upcoming wedding.

Now multiply your **Monthly Disposable Income** figure by the number of months you have until your Wedding Day to get your **Initial Achievable Budget** (assuming there are no other contributors and that you don't take on any debt).

The equation looks like this:

Monthly Disposable Income X (months until your wedding day)

= Initial Achievable Budget

Initial Achievable Budget	

I am going to a hazard a guess that this is significantly less than you anticipated your wedding will cost.

Chapter Two –
The Expenditure
Cull

Don't start crying just yet. All is not lost. When setting our initial budget, I went through the exact same exercise and I realised that if we wanted the wedding we had always dreamed of, then something SERIOUSLY needed to change.

So, I went through our expenditure list and asked myself two questions:

1: *What can we do to reduce some of our expenditure?*

2: *What expenditure could we eliminate altogether?*

You'd be incredibly surprised what you can do to reduce or eliminate some of your expenditure, and in so doing, dramatically increase your **Monthly Disposable Income**.

I am now going to show you the numbers that my husband and I came up with when we did this exercise for ourselves, and then I will show you the result of our expenditure culling exercise.

Armed with what you have learned from my Expenditure Cull, I would like you to do the exact same thing. But I'll talk more about that later on.

Aliesha's Numbers Before The Expenditure Cull

Your Take Home Income p/m	£600
Your Partner's Take Home Income p/m	£1,750
Total Monthly Household Income:	£2,350

Standard Household Expenses	
Mortgage / Rent	£660
Council Tax	£140
Home Insurance	£16
Heating, Power & Water	£120
Home Phone & Broadband	£30
TV Licence & Subscriptions (inc. streaming services)	£40
Car Insurance & Tax	£180
Fuel for the Car(s)	£100
Groceries	£250
Mobile Phone Contracts	£70
Finance / Loan Payments	£160
Credit Card Payments	N/A
Child Care, Nursery & Pre-School	N/A
Commuting Expenses (train, bus, etc)	£40

Health (prescriptions, dentist, etc)	£10
Pets (pet insurance, vet bills, etc)	£30
General Household Expenses (window cleaner, maintenance, etc)	£15
Child Maintenance (commitments from previous relationships, if any)	N/A
Subtotal:	£1,861
Additional Lifestyle Expenses	
Entertainment (eating out, cinema, etc)	£100
Takeaways	£50
Luxury Items (clothes, makeup, etc)	£50
Gift Expenditure (Birthdays, Christmas, etc)	£20
Gym Membership	N/A
Habits (smoking, drinking, etc)	N/A
Holidays & Short Breaks	£100
Other miscellaneous	£60
Subtotal:	£380

Total Monthly Expenditure:	£2,241

Let's take a look at my numbers as an example in relation to the sums we talked about earlier:

Total Monthly Household Income	£2,350
Total Monthly Expenditure	£2,241
Monthly Disposable Income:	£109

£2,350 - £2,241

= £109

We started saving for our wedding 18 months before. So, taking our Monthly Disposable Income and multiplying it by months until wedding gives us £1,962… Quite a way from the £30,000 Wedding of our dreams!

Now let's take a look at my numbers after The Expenditure Cull. I have marked the expenses we reduced or eliminated by noting the amount we reduced by in adjacent brackets.

Aliesha's Numbers After The Expenditure Cull

Standard Household Expenses	
Mortgage / Rent	£660
Council Tax	£140
Home Insurance	£16
Heating, Power & Water	£120
Home Phone & Broadband	£30
TV Licence & Subscriptions (inc. streaming services)	*£15 (-£25)*
Car Insurance & Tax	*£90 (£-90)*
Fuel for the Car(s)	*£75 (-£25)*
Groceries	*£200 (-£50)*

Mobile Phone Contracts	£70
Finance / Loan Payments	£160
Credit Card Payments	N/A
Child Care, Nursery & Pre-School	N/A
Commuting Expenses (train, bus, etc)	£40
Health (prescriptions, dentist, etc)	£10
Pets (pet insurance, vet bills, etc)	£30
General Household Expenses (window cleaner, maintenance, etc)	£15
Child Maintenance (commitments from previous relationships, if any)	N/A
Subtotal:	**£1,671 (-£190)**
Additional Lifestyle Expenses	
Entertainment (eating out, cinema, etc)	£25 (-£75)
Takeaways	£0 (-£50)
Luxury Items (clothes, makeup, etc)	£20 (-£30)

Gift Expenditure (Birthdays, Christmas, etc)	£20
Gym Membership	N/A
Habits (smoking, drinking, etc)	N/A
Holidays & Short Breaks	£50 (-£50)
Other miscellaneous	£30 (-£30)
Subtotal:	**£145 (-£235)**
Total Monthly Expenditure:	**£1,816 (-£425)**

Believe it or not, we were able to reduce our monthly expenditure by £425! Every penny of this is added to our **Monthly Disposable Income**.

We now had £534 spare each month to save. Multiply this by months until the Wedding and all of a sudden we have a much healthier £9,612! This is a massive **390% INCREASE** in the funds we have available for our Wedding during the 18 month period.

It is easy for me to give you my numbers as an example, but I want to give you some context on them too. This will help you to understand what we cut, how we cut it and why we cut it.

You can use this for your next exercise where you will be performing your very own Expenditure Cull.

Let's first take a look at my Standard Household Expenses. These are some of the most difficult expenses to reduce or eliminate due to the fact that, most of these are commodities, and you have a commitment to them. Eliminating some of those expenses could land you in hot water, so we need to be realistic with what we can do here.

TV License & Subscriptions

We had a basic Sky TV subscription, Netflix and our compulsory TV License to begin with. We realised that we never really used our Sky subscription and could cope with regular Freeview and Netflix. This reduced this expense area by £25 per month.

Car Insurance & Tax

My husband and I both had our own cars. This seemed a little silly for us since I use the train to get to work and my husband worked from home. We didn't *need* two cars. So we sold my husband's car and HALVED our motoring expenses, saving us £90 every month.

Fuel for the Car

Due partially to the fact we then only had one car to run, this reduced the amount of fuel required. We also made a point of walking to certain destinations when we didn't really have to drive. This knocked off a further £25 per month.

Groceries

We were able to cut £50 per month from our grocery bill with two simple tricks. Firstly, we started buying the Supermarket's own brand, as opposed to the leading brand of products (we literally noticed zero difference in the quality of the food). Secondly, I stopped buying alcohol. Neither my husband nor I are big drinkers, but, we would have the odd bottle of wine here and there. Think about it this way: if you buy one bottle of wine per week at £5 per bottle, that equates to £390 over an eighteen month period. That would cover a big chunk of your Church or Registrar's fee!

Totaling all of the savings from our **Standard Household Expenses** gives us an extra £190 **Monthly Disposable Income.**

Now let's take a look at our **Additional Lifestyle Expenses**. If you are serious about having the biggest budget possible for your wedding, the **Additional Lifestyle Expenses** area is where you can really reap the rewards of The Expenditure Cull.

Entertainment & Eating Out

I love a good meal out. Since having children, my husband and I rarely go to the cinema or anything like that. However, we would usually spend £100 each month on eating out.

Although we weren't prepared to stop eating out all together, we decided to compromise and instead have just one meal out each month (instead of the one meal per week as we previously had). We actually found that we were more excited about our one meal out each month and enjoyed it all the more. This shaved another £75 from our monthly expenditure.

Takeaways

We cut out takeaways entirely. They're bad for your health, expensive and always make you feel rubbish after eating them anyway. We saved another £50 a month here.

Luxury Items

Our Luxury Items expenditure wasn't particularly high before The Expenditure Cull. But, we were able to cut this significantly by simply asking ourselves *"Do I really need this?"* before buying a new pair of shoes or another mascara. We saved a total of £30 a month by doing this.

Holidays & Short Breaks

Like most people, we have an annual holiday. Usually, we would go away to an all inclusive hotel abroad for a week. While saving for our wedding, we decided to holiday in a static caravan on the East Coast of England for a week. We shared the caravan with my parents. This dramatically affected our holiday expenditure and enabled us to reduce it by half saving us another £50 per month.

Other Miscellaneous

For me, this included the odd Iced Caramel Latte from Costa, among other sweet treats and indulgences. I vowed to cut them out altogether, and instead, make my own at home if I couldn't fight the cravings. This wiped another £30 from our monthly expenditure. Not to mention the benefits to my waistline too!

Chapter Three – Your Expenditure Cull

Now it's back over to you! You've seen what's possible if you really think about it. Using the table on the next page, rewrite your monthly expenditure based on what you could reduce or eliminate in the future.

As before, I would highly recommend getting your partner involved in this exercise. He might not be willing to cancel his Sky Sports subscription so you can have canapes at the wedding.

Standard Household Expenses	
Mortgage / Rent	
Council Tax	
Home Insurance	
Heating, Power & Water	
Home Phone & Broadband	
TV Licence & Subscriptions (inc. streaming services)	
Car Insurance & Tax	
Fuel for the Car/s	
Groceries	
Mobile Phone Contracts	
Finance / Loan Payments	
Credit Card Payments	
Child Care, Nursery & Pre-School	
Commuting Expenses (train, bus, etc)	
Health (prescriptions, dentist, etc)	
Pets (pet insurance, vet bills, etc)	

General Household Expenses (window cleaner, maintenance, etc)	
Child Maintenance (commitments from previous relationships, if any)	
NEW Subtotal:	
Additional Lifestyle Expenses	
Entertainment (eating out, cinema, etc)	
Takeaways	
Luxury Items (clothes, makeup, etc)	
Gift Expenditure (Birthdays, Christmas, etc)	
Gym Membership	
Habits (smoking, drinking, etc)	
Holidays & Short Breaks	
Other miscellaneous	
NEW Subtotal:	
NEW Total Monthly Expenditure:	

Now that you've got that bit out of the way (It's painful, I know, but it'll all be worth it!), we can revise your **Monthly Disposable Income** and workout how much more you'll have to contribute to the budget.

Take your **Total Monthly Household Income** and subtract your *NEW* **Total Monthly Expenditure**, then multiply that by the months until the Wedding. This number, your **Revised Achievable Budget**, is what you can potentially save between now and your Wedding Day.

The equation looks like this:

(Total Monthly Household Income

– New Total Monthly Expenditure)

X Months Until The Wedding

= Revised Achievable Budget

My Revised Achievable Budget	

TIP: *It is easy to write these numbers down, but to make it a reality you've actually got to stick to it. Between the two of you, help each other to stay on track. You make a great team!*

Now that we know what the potential scope of your savings are between now and your wedding day, we can add that to any amounts received or promised by contributors and any other savings you, yourself, may be contributing to the wedding fund.

The total is your **Budget**.

I'd love to know how much extra funds you were able to make available with this exercise! Be sure to let me know in the **Busy Bride To Be** Facebook Group.

Chapter Four –
Budget Allocation

Now, unless you organise weddings for a living, it is unlikely that you've planned anything on the scale of what you are about to embark on. It is also likely to be the largest event you ever plan.

Many Brides-to-Be feel intimidated by this fact. They look at their Budget and ask themselves, "Now what?". They don't know how much of their Budget should be allocated to which part of their plan. If you are feeling like this, don't worry... you're not alone. And anyway, I'm here to help you through it.

My Budget Allocation

Using my own Budget of £15,000 as an example, I am going to show you what proportion of the Budget each area of the average Wedding is allocated to.

Example Wedding Budget Allocation		
Function	Proportion	Amount
Catering	35%	£5,250
Venue	15%	£2,250
Photography & Video	10%	£1,500
Dress & Attire	10%	£1,500
Music & Entertainment	9%	£1,350
Flowers & Decor	9%	£1,350
Ceremony	5%	£750
Stationary	3%	£450
Gifts	2%	£300
Transport	2%	£300
Totals	**100%**	**£15,000**

Remember these numbers are only average figures, not something you *must* stick to. Simply use them as a guide, and they will help you to make informed decisions when you speak to vendors and suppliers later on.

My own actual spend was slightly different to the average breakdown, so don't be worried if yours is too. Here is roughly what mine looked like:

Aliesha's Wedding Budget Allocation		
Function	**Proportion**	**Amount**
Catering	50.7%	£7,590
Venue	20%	£3,000
Music & Entertainment	2%	£320
Dress & Attire	11.5%	£1,731
Photography & Video	5.8%	£860
Flowers & Decor	2.5%	£375
Ceremony	3.5%	£524
Stationary	1%	£145
Gifts	3%	£452
Transport	0%	£0.00
Totals	**100%**	**£14,997**

As you can see, my own budget allocation proportion percentages are quite different in places. As you'll find out later in the book, I saved quite a lot on my "Flowers & Decor", which was extra money we used for our Venue and Catering.

Your Budget Allocation

It's back over to you again now. Using the Budget you established for yourself earlier on, fill in the table on the next page with your own breakdown.

The equation looks like this:

$$(\text{Proportion}/100)$$

$$\text{X Total Budget}$$

$$= \text{Amount}$$

For example, here is our catering calculation:

$$(35/100)$$

$$\text{X } 15,000$$

$$= 5,250$$

TIP: *Use an online calculator to help calculate your budget allocation - percentagecalculator.net.*

Your Wedding Budget Allocation		
Function	**Proportion**	**Amount**
Catering	35%	
Venue	15%	
Photography & Video	10%	
Dress & Attire	10%	
Music & Entertainment	9%	
Flowers & Decor	9%	
Ceremony	5%	
Stationary	3%	
Gifts	2%	
Transport	2%	
Totals	**100%**	

Ultimately, there is no right or wrong way to allocate your Budget. This is, after all, *your* wedding day, and it should be about what you want.

Chapter Five – Budget Enhancing Tools

Now we get on to the really fun part of making your Budget stretch loads further than it really should.

In the introduction, I told you about how my Wedding should have cost £30,000, but we managed to pay only a little under £15,000 for everything, even though I got married on a Saturday in August (peak season).

I forgive you for feeling suspicious of my rather big claim. When I think about it myself, it sounds pretty crazy. But I promise you it happened. It can happen for you too.

You see, I implemented certain tactics and strategies that enabled me to knock significant amounts of money from the price tag of pretty much every product or service for my wedding. I even got some things thrown in for free too!

I am going to expose to you the secrets that the Wedding Industry doesn't want you to know about planning your Wedding under budget **without** compromising on what you want.

I highly recommend you take notes to help this to sink in better. So, let's get started.

To help make some of these strategies work to their highest potential, wherever possible for each requirement of your wedding, try and have at least three different suppliers who can undertake the task. Ideally, they should all be fairly evenly priced and offer a very similar level of service.

For each different area of your wedding, I have included several different money saving strategies you could employ. Not every strategy may be applicable to your situation, so think carefully on which ones to use.

Remember to be polite, reasonable and confident in your delivery of these tactics and you should be able to shave a considerable sum from your costs.

Money Saving Strategies

I want to begin by talking you through all of the different strategies you could use to help reduce the cost of different parts of your wedding.

In some cases, these strategies wielded together may be even more powerful still. You might even be disappointed at how simple some of these strategies are, but you'd be surprised about how few people actually use them.

I like to think of these strategies as tools. Each tool is best suited for one particular job. For example, the tool you use to save money on your venue may not be as effective for getting a discount on your photographer.

Once you know what these tools are, we will talk about how to apply them to the specific areas of your wedding to help get you the best possible outcome.

Just Ask

It is a common belief that asking for a discount is rude or cheeky. The opposite is true. I have found that suppliers *expect* you to ask for a discount, and so have priced their products or services accordingly, in order to accommodate a discount *if* you ask for it. My husband has always told me, "Never to accept the first offer."

There are multiple ways to ask for a discount, and how you ask will very much depend on which supplier you are asking.

A "one size fits all" way to ask could be something like this: "What can you do to lower the cost for us?". It works very well since you are not asking permission for a discount; you are communicating that you expect some sort of discount. They can't simply say, "no" to that question like they could if you asked, "Any chance of a discount?" This strategy is most effective when delivered politely, but assertively, and with confidence. Don't feel guilty, they can still always tell you there's nothing they could do on the price.

It is important to have already received a quote of some sort before you ask for a discount.

Get a Breakdown

I noticed that many of the suppliers I approached "packaged" their products and services. More often than not, these packages included things that I either didn't want or had a preference on something slightly different to that which was being offered.

In this circumstance, I would ask for a breakdown of exactly what is included so that you can identify things that you could leave out.

If you find something you don't want or need, then ask the supplier, "How much less could you do it for if we didn't have the _____?"
Once again, you are not asking for permission. The ball is in the supplier's court, and you'll find them surprisingly accommodating in order to secure your business.

If a supplier is not willing to reduce the cost of their package, ask them to substitute certain parts for things that you do want or need. More on this later.

Payment Terms

Since you will likely be talking to your suppliers about hiring their services quite some time in advance, you can often leverage payment terms in order to get an extra discount.

By offering to pay either a larger deposit, or even the full balance up front, it can motivate suppliers to be more flexible on their pricing.

Due to the increased risk this may expose you to, it's a good idea to purchase Wedding Insurance as early as possible. Be sure to get a receipt for any payments made and where possible, pay on a Credit Card for added protection.

Play Them Against Each Other

Earlier, I suggested that you should aim to have at least three different potential suppliers for each product or service you require. As before, they should all provide a very similar level of service and should all be similarly priced. This makes it very easy to play them against each other.

To do so, you'd get an initial quote from each of them. Then ask, "What can you do to lower the cost for us?", and get that sent over to you as a written quote. Take the cheapest of all the quotes and ask the other suppliers to beat that price to secure your custom.

Mailing Lists

Where possible, get yourself signed up to email lists of potential suppliers to ensure you are among the first to find out about any last minute deals, cancellations and special offers.

Simply by being on our chosen venue's email list, we were able to score a £5,000 discount, but more on this later on.

Cancellations & Last Minute

This is a strategy that will not apply to everyone, especially if you are planning your wedding well in advance. However, if you are prepared to gamble on your desired wedding date, you can quite often get a significant discount.

You don't want to leave booking everything until the last minute, because procrastinating booking it all for the same date could prove to be very challenging and will add unnecessary stress.

Out of Season

The wedding season is recognised to run from May through to October. During the season, expect to pay more than you would with a winter wedding, excluding Christmas, New Year and Valentine's day, which are also extremely popular dates that get booked well in advance.

In terms of days of the week, Saturday is usually the most expensive, followed by Friday and then Sunday. To obtain the best discount consider a Monday - Thursday Wedding.

Coupled with the fact that summertime is when most people take their annual holidays, you shouldn't have any concerns about your guests getting the time off work if you book well enough in advance.

Get It Thrown In

If haggling on the price gets you nowhere, there is another way to get a deal: get value added for free. Ask them to throw in an additional product or related service for free if you agree to their price. This should always be something that is on your list that you would otherwise need to pay for.

This strategy is most effective when you are ready to commit. Use it like this: "If you can throw in the House DJ, I am happy to pay you a deposit right now". This will show the supplier that you mean business and that you are not just going to go away and think on it. You'll find that people are a little more flexible when you dangle money in front of them.

Chapter Six –
Tools In Actions

Now that you have a better idea of the different ways you can approach saving money for the various different requirements of your wedding, let's look at each supplier and some recommendations of how to implement the strategies against them.

But first, here are a few things *not* to do when implementing these strategies:

- Don't try to justify asking for a discount. Believe me when I say that suppliers will have heard every tale there is as to why you deserve a discount. The fact is, *why* does not matter and will generally result in a lower discount than if you hadn't tried to justify it.

- Don't be rude. Always be polite and considerate in your dealings with suppliers regardless of whether they offer you a discount or not.

- Don't be unreasonable. Behaving in an unreasonable manner is not going to help you get what you want. Always be reasonable and understanding, and it will go a long way to helping you secure a better deal.

Save Money on Your Venue

My husband and I fell in love with the very first venue we visited, a beautiful Manor House in heart of the Suffolk countryside.

At this time we were still a long way from actually booking anything, but we wanted to get some venue ideas as early as possible. We attended an open day the venue was holding. Before leaving, we got a quote from one of the sales representatives.

The quote totaled just over £20,000 and included the following:

- Exclusive venue hire for the day

- Three-course wedding breakfast

- Evening Food

- Reception Drinks

- Table Wine & Toasting Drink

- Overnight accommodation and breakfast at the Manor for selected guests

- Giant garden games

- Sweet cart

- Canapes

- House DJ

- Chair covers

- Centerpieces

I can honestly say that the number was a little daunting, even though I hadn't even put a budget down on paper yet.

One of the main reasons this venue appealed to us so much was due to the fact that they had 14 bedrooms in which some of our guests could stay, so I got myself on the venue's email list, as they told me that I could be notified about any cancellations as they became available.

On Valentine's weekend of 2017, my venue was running a special deal on some of the remaining available dates for that year. I was a little surprised to see a Saturday in

Mid-August available (considering this is exactly what I was hoping for).

The special rate was for the exclusive hire of the venue for the day, food and drink for our daytime guests, and food for evening guests.

Totaled, it was £9,000, whereas the usual rate for this date should have been £14,500.

The total cost of hiring all of the rooms (which included a buffet style breakfast in the morning) was £2,750. However, if you booked all of them at once, the venue would do a special rate of £2,000.

There were also two other offerings that the venue had that we were hoping to book: their resident DJ and the giant garden games. The cost of these two services would add an additional £550.

So, with £9,000 for the venue hire, food and drink plus the overnight accommodation, DJ and giant garden games we were now looking at a grand total of £11,550. In all honesty, considering the massive discount we had already got I was tempted to just say "BOOK US IN!".

But, I thought I would try pushing for a little extra discount by offering our commitment and an immediate deposit payment if they would agree to a total price of £10,000.

The venue responded saying that they couldn't possibly do all of that for £10,000 and that instead they could do it for £11,000. My husband suggested we offer that we would meet them in the middle at £10,500. To my amazement they agreed! We ended up paying £10,500 for what should have been £17,800.

This means that by implementing some of the simple strategies we talked about earlier, we were able to save a MASSIVE £7,300. We, therefore, made more funds available to be spent on other parts of our Big Day. While, admittedly, I did feel a little awkward pushing for more money off because of the fact that I knew I was already getting an amazing deal, boy am I glad that I did!

However awkward you might feel, it is certainly worth it when you save big and give yourself more money to play with later on down the line.

When I first set out on my wedding planning journey, I vowed to myself that no matter our budget, I would not compromise on what I wanted. I would remind myself of this every time I felt like just taking the first offer.

Save Money on Your Photographer

As we established earlier on in the book, your photography costs will account for roughly 10% of your Budget. It would be nice if we could get it down to somewhere around the 7-8% mark, wouldn't it?

Start by considering exactly what you want from your photos:

⊛ Do you want photos of the getting ready, ceremony, group photos, first dance, cake cutting and evening reception?

⊛ Do you want digital images or would you like prints, canvases, etc too?

⊛ Would you like the same images taken from multiple angles or are you satisfied with a single angle? (Multiple angles means photographers plus their assistants and so higher costs.)

For most couples, the most important photos are of the ceremony, group photos, first dance and cake cutting. Consider which parts of the day you would most like to have the professional photographs of, and which you would be happy with guest photos of. If you elect to have guests take some photos, make sure to officially ask them if they would do you the honour of capturing some snaps throughout the course of the day. Most people are extremely pleased to be chosen to perform this role. Ideal candidates could be one of the Groomsmen, Bridesmaids, a budding Student Photographer amongst your guests, etc.

My cousin, a keen hobbyist photographer, captured some absolutely BEAUTIFUL photographs at my wedding. Many of which made it into our Wedding Album.

Keep in mind, the more time your photographer is at your wedding, the more photos they are going to take. The more photos they take, the more photos they are going to have to edit. The more photos they have to edit, the more they are going to charge you.

For my wedding, I had my photographer stay until after the first dance and cake cutting, and then relied on photos taken by my guests for the reception.

Using a Wedding Hashtag is a great idea for ensuring that you are able to find all of the photos your guests upload from your wedding to social media sites like Facebook, Instagram and Twitter. After the wedding you can search the hashtag and download all of the ones you like and add them to your album.

I didn't do this myself, although, it is in hindsight something I wish I had. I've been to a few weddings since my own and they all made use of the hashtag and it worked really well for them.

Most photographers offer slightly different packages for weddings. The more expensive packages tend to include things like personalised prints, canvases and photo books. While these are all very nice, chances are that they are ordering them from the very same online printing companies that you could order from yourself with the only difference being that you are paying a middleman (your photographer) an additional fee.

I would recommend opting for digital photos only, and then having prints, canvases and photo books created by yourself. These websites are super easy to use, and they often include tools that allow you to apply filters to images such as black and white or sepia if you'd prefer.

Much of a photographer's business relies on referrals from past or existing customers. There are a couple of ways that you could use this to your advantage:

1: Refer a friend who is engaged to wed and is currently looking for a photographer.

Use any photos you might have from your engagement shoot (if you had one). You can post these on social media with an accompanying comment such as; "Our photos from our Engagement Shoot have come out BEAUTIFULLY! Let me know if you're looking for a fantastic Wedding Photographer and I'll put you in touch".

If you agree a referral rate with your photographer, this can help to shave a chunk of money from your final bill.

2: Offer to place discreet advertising for your photographer on your wedding day.

It need only be something like a business card or small leaflet on each table. This can be effective at catching the attention of any engaged-to-wed guests you have that enjoy your photographer's style and might be interested in talking further with them.

Save Money on Music & Entertainment

Regardless of whether you are having a DJ, band, singer, comedian (see my Wedding Ideas & Inspiration book for a complete list of ideas), etc you can save some money if you go about things the right way.

Side Note: *Wedding Ideas & Inspiration book is a part of the Ultimate Wedding Planning Pack you get FREE when you join BusyBrideClub.com*

Because bands hired through regular entertainment agencies are generally pretty pricey, I would always start by looking at who you know first. In your network of friends and family, is there anyone who boasts the talent you are looking to hire out? More often than not, a friend or family member would be proud to be asked to perform at your wedding and would likely not charge a lot, if anything at all!

You could also consider contacting local colleges and universities and ask if they have a band they hire out for events. The fees for such bands are rarely anywhere near what you might pay for a professional band.

Frequent some of your local pubs and bars where they host live bands and see if any take your fancy. Approach them and ask if they would play at your wedding. You might be surprised at how little some might charge you.

Lastly, keep a look out for professional buskers and street musicians. I have seen some amazingly talented people performing on the streets for loose change. I would bet that many of these people would jump at the chance to play at your wedding. Negotiating a fair rate both parties are happy with should be easy.

Save Money on Dress & Attire

Dress and attire generally includes your wedding dress, Bridesmaid dresses and suits for The Groom, Best Man, Groomsmen, Father of the Bride and Father of the Groom.

There are numerous ways in which you can cut the expenses with Dress and Attire. So, to begin with, let's discuss what you can do to save money on your wedding dress.

Having been a Bride myself, I know that the wedding dress is one of the most important parts of the entire day. Getting the dress right is imperative. I, myself, spent many hours in many different bridal shops trying to find "The One".

Typically, a wedding dress is worn only for the one single day and will spend the rest of its life in your spare room or in the loft. With that being said, would it matter to you if your wedding dress had already been worn by someone else? Especially if it meant saving as much as 90% off the original price tag?

That's right, I'm talking about buying a pre-owned wedding dress. Your guests would be none the wiser that what you are wearing is in fact a second hand bridal gown.

Not for you? Fair enough! But for those of you who would be willing to wear a pre-owned dress, here are some places you can find them:

1   Charity Shops - There is a charity shop in my local town that, during the wedding

season, will display pre-owned wedding dresses in the front window. I have noticed the prices starting at less than £100. Not only would you be able to grab a bargain, but you'd be supporting a great cause at the same time. Win, Win.

2   Facebook Groups - There are Facebook Groups that have been created specifically for the resale of pre-owned wedding dresses.

3   Resale Websites - There are countless websites that specialise in the resale of used bridal gowns. A quick Google search for "second hand wedding dresses" resulted in me finding www.stillwhite.co.uk which, at the time of my visit, had over 27,000 wedding dresses for sale directly from newlywed brides. I have no affiliation to this site, and there are, of course, many others like it.

You might also consider trying some of the well known marketplaces people use to sell second hand goods on such as eBay, Gumtree, Preloved, etc.

The fact that newlywed brides are selling their used wedding dresses brings about another point: you too can sell yours when you're finished with it. Granted, this doesn't help with your upfront expenses, but will help you to recover some later on down the line.

If you would rather not buy second hand, but still want to get a significant discount on your dress you could consider buying a former display or sample dress from a bridal store.

Most bridal stores will have an "End of Season Sale", where they sell off at a discount all of the sample dresses for the previous season's designs in order to make way for new designs. This is a great time to get a bargain.

This is, in fact, how I got my £1,599 wedding dress for just £399 - a fraction of the original price. That cost did not include alterations, but I had these done by an independent seamstress for an extra £180. I still got the dress of my dreams for less than half of the original cost.

Just because there is no end of season sale on at the time, it doesn't mean that you can't ask to buy the sample for a discount. It is quite commonplace, and you will find many bridal stores are happy to accommodate you in this way.

This leads us nicely on to simply asking for a discount. We have already discussed how to ask for a discount earlier on in the book. Use the "Just Ask" strategy we talked about to try and get a discount. If the supplier is not willing to budge on the price, but you are sold on the dress you could always try and get them to throw something in for free such as a veil, hoop or petticoat, shoes, tiara or hair accessories.

If you have no intention of keeping your wedding dress once the Big Day is over, then you could always consider renting one. You can rent a dress from as little as £100. By renting, you potentially have access to more expensive designer dresses too, which might otherwise be outside of your price range. Renting however does mean that you would be unable to have adjustments made.

That's your wedding dress taken care of. Now, let's talk about how to save money on the remaining outfits for those in the Bridal Party.

It is a myth that everything should match and be uniformed with a wedding. In fact, it is a recent trend to have mismatching Bridesmaid dresses and Groomsmen suits etc. If your theme is flexible, you could consider asking some or all of the Bridal Party to wear something that they already own (with your seal of approval of course). Most, if not all men have a suit of some description in their wardrobes. The same goes for ladies with dresses. I would be very surprised if the ladies did not have something that would be perfectly suitable too.

If you would rather have a little more control over the outfits, you could ask people to buy their own outfits. I know, it sounds a little cheeky at first. But, if you think about it, nearly everyone else who will be attending your wedding will be buying themselves a new outfit to wear anyway. You might even find that some people will outright offer to pay for their own outfit. My advice? Take them up on it. Thank them and explain how helpful that would be at keeping your costs down.

If you do ask people to buy their own outfit, make sure to involve them in the process (I did only say "a little more control", not "complete control"). You need to make sure that they are not buying something that they would never wear again or that they don't like.

Also, make sure that what you are expecting them to buy is not unnecessarily expensive. If you are unsure what an unreasonably expensive outfit might be, ask yourself how much you would be willing to pay for if the roles were reversed and you were buying your own outfit for someone else's wedding.

Where possible, try and buy or rent as many outfits and complimentary accessories from as few suppliers as possible. By bringing more business to one supplier, you are more likely to be able to negotiate a discount.

For my wedding, we hired the suits, all from the same supplier, for the following: The

Groom, Best Man, Usher, Father of the Bride and Father of the Groom. This resulted in us being able to get the Groom's suit (the most expensive one) thrown in for free!

Accessories are great things to use to seal the deal where discounts are not achievable. I talked about this earlier regarding The Dress. If you can't get a discount, try and get something thrown in for free that you would otherwise have to pay for. This is especially easy when hiring, as there is no real additional cost to the supplier.

With suits you could get ties, cravats, cufflinks, buttonholes, etc thrown in. With dresses you could get shoes, jewellery, headpieces, etc to sweeten the deal.

Just to remind you once again, *never* take the first offer without first attempting to get a discount or some added value free.

Save Money on Flowers & Decor

The potential scope of flowers and decor is huge. You need to draw a line somewhere and stick to it.

Depending upon your venue, you are likely to need some decor as a minimum. But there are many beautiful venues out there that barely need any decorating at all. Just some discreet details to make it your own and you can be done with. Pay attention to this when you are looking around at venues. Finding somewhere that requires less decor is going to save you money.

Beg, borrow (just don't steal). Chances are that you know someone who is newly wed. They may still have a treasure trove full of, now redundant, wedding decor just waiting to be made use of again. Pick out the bits that would suit your Big Day and ask to borrow them. Maybe they are not prepared to lend them to you (I get it, things could get broken or go missing), so you could offer to buy them. Assuming they are not being held on to as a keepsake, I think you'll find most newlywed brides will be happy to get rid of the stuff now cluttering their homes.

Have you thought about doing it yourself? I know it takes up more of your precious time, but I personally really enjoyed creating most of my flowers and decor myself. I enlisted the help of Mum for a few projects and my Bridesmaids for others. We made an evening of it with a movie and a bottle of wine. I made all of my own bouquets, flowers and buttonholes, as well as my centerpieces and other decorative pieces.

The single most rewarding thing was seeing my creations all together and in place on the day of the wedding and hearing my guests gush over them, saying things like, "Wow, these must have cost a fortune", or ; "Who was your florist? I want to book them for my wedding".

Decide early on whether to have flowers or not... Yes, that's right. You don't *need* to have flowers. In fact, it is becoming more and more common for people *not* to have flowers.

If you decide to keep the flowers, here are some ideas to help you to keep the cost as low as possible:

1. Buy local and seasonal. Got your heart set on Poinsettias for a Summer wedding? Not only are they from USA and Mexico, but they are Winter flowers. This means that you should expect to pay a premium for such flowers. Try and stick to flowers in season that are available locally; this will help keep the price down.

2   Go for faux. The untrained eye would struggle to distinguish the difference between false flowers and real flowers. Not to mention the fact that fake flowers are substantially cheaper than real flowers, and can be sold on once you have finished with them.

3   Stick to as few types as possible. If you settle on real flowers, try and stick to as few different flowers as you can, ideally no more than two. The more you have of one type of flower, the bigger the discount your florist will be able to get from their wholesaler, which they can in turn pass on to you.

4   Use greenery to bulk out your displays. In the natural world of plants and flowers, greenery is in abundance. So why should it not play a part in your flower displays for your

wedding? Displays on a budget can be made to look amazing simply by padding them out with some cleverly placed greenery.

TIP: *Waste not. Got spare flowers left over? Using a pair of scissors, chop the petals into a container to be used as confetti.*

Save Money on The Ceremony

Let's take a look at the ceremony itself in terms where the money is spent. The 5% you should allow in your budget accommodates purely for the hire of a registrar or celebrant. If you are having a church wedding, you will likely be hiring a priest or vicar.

If you have an official registrar whose presence and signature officiates the marriage on the day of the wedding, they are provided by your local authority's registry office. The fee they charge is set by your local authority and varies by region. Because of this, there is no negotiating prices (trust me, we tried).

In order to cut the costs, you could hire a celebrant. Celebrants are authorised individuals who will conduct your ceremony modelled to your design (within reason). They are usually self-employed, or part of an agency and so prices can be flexible.

For your marriage to be official, you would still need to follow up with a ceremony at your local registry office with prices starting from around £45, depending upon region.

For church weddings, the church will supply a priest or vicar to conduct the ceremony for you. Once again, the price is 100% negotiable. Some people feel guilty about negotiating prices with their Church... Don't!

If possible, having your ceremony and reception at the same venue can save you big bucks. Otherwise, you will be forking out for two separate venues. Not to mention the inconvenience of having to travel between the two part way through the day.

More and more venues are acquiring the required license for people to be wed on their property - just be sure to check this with your chosen venue before you commit to anything. Also, clarify that the license has been granted and is not pending application. Since there are very strict rules and requirements a venue must adhere to in order to be granted the license, not all applications are successful.

As with most other services wedding related, getting hitched on a weekday will once again save you money on your ceremony. It is commonplace for everyone's fees to be more expensive on those days with higher demand (Friday, Saturday and Sunday).

Save Money on Stationery

It is *really* easy to go overboard on your wedding stationery costs. When you first get started, you are going to want to send out "Save the Dates", the invites, RSVP cards, place names, etc.

I have noticed that most people tend to spend a large proportion of their stationary budget on the invitations alone. This is down to the fact that they believe that by their choice of invitation, they are setting the expectation for the day itself. So a grander invitation equals a grander wedding day.

Don't get caught in this trap. It simply doesn't exist. It is born out of the need for everything to be "perfect". The quality of your invitation will likely go totally unnoticed by most invitees, and so spending vast amounts of money on amazing invitations is unwise. That money could be far better spent elsewhere.

There are hundreds of websites you can purchase printed invitations from for a reasonable price. A simple Google search for "wedding invitations" is a great place to start.

The most cost effective route to wedding stationery is to do it yourself. But this comes at a different cost: your time! If you are a busy working mum like I was when I was planning my wedding, you might be hard pressed to find the time to do this. With that being said, I did in fact DIY all of my wedding stationery - with the help of my Mum and my bridesmaids.

As I mentioned before, I booked my venue on a last minute deal, and so I had to be flexible on dates. Because I booked six months before my wedding, I skipped "Save the Dates" and went straight to invitations.

I like to keep things simple - my invitations were literally put together using the Google

Docs word processor (Google's free online version of Microsoft Word). I bought some coloured card from my local stationers and printed them on my home printer.

They were far from "perfect", but I thought they looked great and they served their purpose well. A few of my guests even commented on how nice they were. I'd be happy to share the template with you. Just drop a message in my Facebook Group and someone will share it with you.

If you need some inspiration on making your own wedding stationery, Pinterest is a great place to start. You can also find bucket loads of tutorials on YouTube.

I didn't use place names for the wedding breakfast. Instead, I doubled up my favors as place names. Each favor had a small kraft paper, handwritten tag tied to it and was put in the correct seat. I also printed our table plans onto card and mounted it onto a large picture frame which stood on an easel outside of the dining room. Our usher helped direct our guests to their seats, while reminding them not to swap seats lest they get the wrong meal (we didn't write out everyone's food choices on cards as the venue staff knew what meal was going to each seat).

Instead of RSVP cards, I did something that did cost me a little extra (about £30), but it saved me a whole lot of time. It was a financial sacrifice I was willing to make considering the time saved. I used an online service to collect my RSVPs. I bought a domain name (e.g. www.ourweddingrsvp.com) and directed that to the RSVP service. On the bottom of each of my invitations I wrote, "Please go to www.ourweddingrsvp.com" (replacing the domain with our actual domain). Once everyone had RSVP'd, I downloaded a spreadsheet and handed it off to my venue.

The reason it saved me so much time was because I loaded all of the meal options into the RSVP software, and also included song requests, transport and accommodation requirements for those of my guests travelling a long way to celebrate with us. It was actually really simple to do. But I have created a free video tutorial on how you can set up your own digital RSVPs, you can find it at www.rsvptutorial.com

If you wanted to take your digital stationery to the next step, you could always use digital invitations too! The very same service I used for the RSVPs caters for invitations.

If you would rather not make your own or use a digital service, that leaves you with two options:

1: Buy off the shelf

2: Have them made for you

The cheapest (by far) is to buy off the shelf stationery. Much like a regular children's birthday party invitation, you fill in the blanks with yours and your future husband's names, the date, venue and any other details you wish to include.

Custom stationery made to order can be a lot more expensive because it takes a lot more time to create and cannot be as easily mass produced as off the shelf alternatives. The more personalisation included on your custom stationery, the more it will cost you. To help keep that cost down limit or leave out personalisation, and add the finishing touches yourself later on. Metallic Sharpie marker pens were my best friends!

A great place to find people who will custom make wedding stationery for a pretty reasonable cost is at craft fairs. Craft fairs are full of artistic and creative individuals touting their wares. You will almost certainly find someone who is selling handmade cards. If you like their style, approach them and negotiate a deal for them to custom make your stationery for you.

I have two final tips to help save money on custom stationery:

Firstly, if you need eighty invitations, order one hundred. You WILL make mistakes when you fill them out, and you WILL invite extra people last minute. It might seem to contradict my previous comments, however, adding extra to original order is a lot cheaper than asking the supplier to start a new job for just a few.

Secondly, be sure to proofread, and proofread again, and again. Get your partner, parents, in-laws, bridesmaids and everyone you can think of to proofread it. Pay close attention to spellings of names and addresses. Dates are also a must to be checked, not just the day and month, but the year too.

One further point I'd like to make is, if you can hand deliver invitations locally, then do! It might not cost much for a single second class stamp, but if you have eighty invitations to send out, that can soon add up to a significant amount! I delivered most of my invitations by hand, not even making special journeys to do so, just by handing them out when I saw people. There are probably going to be some guests that you don't see on a regular basis, but maybe they live nearby and you could pop it through the door on your way past.

Save Money on Gifts

Besides the obvious parts, one of the most rewarding parts of my wedding day was when I was able to thank those who had an integral part to play, those who without, nothing would have been possible.

One of the most traditional ways to do this is with gifts.

Although you might be tempted to splash out on extravagant gifts for those vital people, just remember the old saying: "It's the thought that counts". As is true with stationery, personalised gifts are going to be a lot more expensive than non-personalised. Skipping personalisation on your gifts will really help you to get more value for your money. The costs of gifts can escalate quite quickly as your "thank you" list grows. My own list of thank you's was quite long and so was the gift list.

It was around this time that I got a little despondent shopping for gifts. I just couldn't find anything I liked for a reasonable price. This personal pain led me to open my own online shop selling gifts specifically for the bridal party.

Shameless plug for my shop for those interested: busybridetobe.com/shop

Chapter Seven – Bonus Money Saving Ideas

Revisit Your Guest List

One of the single most effective ways to significantly reduce the cost of your wedding overall is to reconsider your guest list. The number of guests you invite, both for the ceremony and the reception have a direct impact on the cost of pretty much every area of your wedding.

You should only be inviting people who you want to attend your wedding, and not those you feel obliged to invite.

There are a few other things you can do to help reduce your guest list:

1   Would you buy them dinner? I myself was really struggling with my guest list. I confided in a friend who had recently married, and she said to go through everyone on my guest list and ask myself, "Would I buy them

dinner?". If the answer was no, then they got dropped from the list.

2   Consider not inviting children. My husband and I decided only to invite children of whom we had a close relationship with. For us, this mainly consisted of family. We were a little nervous about telling others that their children were not invited, however, we found that most were actually grateful for an excuse to have the time out on their own.

3   Don't invite "plus ones". There is usually that guest who has recently got into a new relationship. You might feel obliged to invite these new partners to accompany your guests, however, you absolutely do not need to. You might find they later ask if their partner can also attend, these

you can consider on a case by case situation.

4   Put some guests on a reserve list. If there some people you would like to attend your wedding, but your budget or other restrictions (such as venue capacity, etc) can't accommodate it, put them on a reserve list. You may find that some of your invited guests are unable to attend, at which point your reserve guests can fill their seats.

Buy Rather Than Hire

If budget allows, buy, use and sell afterwards.

Quite often, you'll even find that certain items are actually cheaper to buy rather than hire. When we were planning our wedding, we originally looked at hiring centerpieces. The prices varied, but most were around £40 - £50 per table. We had seven round tables, plus our top table, so were looking at between £300 and £400 for centerpieces alone. That was quite a bit more than we were hoping to spend just on centerpieces. So I did some research online and visited wedding fairs to get ideas; then I went along to my local craft stores to see what I could find in there. My mum and I spent some time in various different shops, putting things together to see how they looked.

Eventually, I decided on simple centerpieces which consisted of silk flowers arranged in a jar, which I decorated with hessian and lace, and sat on a mirrored plate. I then filled the jars with pearls and scattered a few pearls onto the mirrored plates. I was so pleased with the end result of our centerpieces. They were simple but pretty and each centerpiece cost us less than £10!

Although I did spend some time putting the centerpieces together, we made a pretty decent saving, and I got so much satisfaction on the Big Day when our guests complimented them. So it was well worth the time spent in the evenings once my children were in bed.

Not only did we buy our centerpieces, but we also bought the rest of our decorations instead of hiring them. This included lanterns down the aisle, which we picked up for about £6 each and decorated with pink roses, a hessian banner for the top table and all of our signs, including one for the guest book, one for the sweet table and one for the ceremony seating plan.

For the signs, I bought plain white canvases, then used metallic sharpies to write on them. I then used the leftover flowers from the lanterns to decorate them. They cost me less than £5 each to make. Originally, I found a sign which said 'choose a seat, not a side' that I liked which was £40!

Something else we decided against hiring out was a sweet cart. We were quoted £200 for the cart, sweets, bags and tongs. Instead we bought large plastic jars, bags, tongs and scoops for under £20 and then spent £50 on sweets at our local wholesaler. This obviously did not include the actual sweet cart, but we placed the jars on the table next to our guest book and they still looked really nice after we had decorated the table with a sign and a garland.

On top of all that, once our wedding was over, we sold everything we didn't have any use for. This included our centerpieces, some of the decorations, signs and sweet jars. We managed to make back just over £100 by selling some of our unwanted stuff. Now that's not a lot in the grand scheme of things, but that's £100 we wouldn't have had if we had hired everything instead of bought it.

Photo booths usually cost around the £400 mark to hire for a few hours. Have you thought about doing your own? This can be done fairly cheaply. All you need is an area in your venue to set up a backdrop, a few props and a camera set up on a tripod. And there you have it, a DIY photo booth! Alternatively, if your venue doesn't have the space or you want to save even more money, just get some props on sticks and leave them somewhere for your guests to take their own pictures on their phones. They can then share all their pictures with you afterwards.

Chair cover hire can vary drastically, from as little as £1 per chair to as much as £5 per chair and even more if you're having sashes too. If you shop around, you can actually buy the chair covers and sashes for a very similar price as hiring them. Once you've used them, as long as they are in good condition still, you are likely to make most of your money back by selling them. The only thing you have to consider is that you will have to fit them yourself.

You might even be lucky enough to not need chair covers. My husband and I originally planned on having chair covers, but our venues chairs were so pretty, it seemed a shame to cover them - we didn't even need sashes.

Post boxes are very popular to hire, and although they can sometimes be hired relatively cheaply, they can be bought for almost the same price, if not less. Simple cardboard post boxes can be picked up for as little as a few quid, and you can always decorate your own if you can't find one you like.

You can also hire table numbers. But again, these are probably cheaper to buy, depending on what you want. I bought freestanding wooden numbers on eBay and painted them how I wanted them, but you can find some really lovely table numbers that don't require you doing any DIY cheap enough. Once again, these can be sold on afterwards.

A lot of people choose to hire suits. This is usually the most cost effective option.

However, you can pick up some lovely suits in high street sales at very reasonable prices. If your husband is likely to wear it again, this would be a good option. Otherwise you could sell it after the big day.

Single Supplier Discounts

Make the most of volume discounts by buying or hiring more from one single supplier. For example, if you are hiring chair covers from a supplier, they will more often than not offer other services, like centerpieces, decorations or maybe even a sweet cart. If any of the services that they offer are on your list, ask the supplier for a discount. The more you get, the higher the discount could be.

Some places will even throw in freebies to encourage you to spend more. Use this in your favour. You should make sure the freebies are things you want and need, otherwise you won't really be making any savings.

Shop around for similar deals, and even if the store does not advertise that kind of deal, it doesn't mean you can't ask.

Getting more from one supplier can work in your favour in lots of scenarios. The following are a few examples:

⊛ If you're having your hair and makeup done, look for someone who does both. This is likely to be cheaper than paying two separate people.

⊛ When buying your dress, consider getting your shoes, hair accessories and bridesmaid dresses from the same shop for a larger discount.

⊛ The same as with your wedding dress, when getting the men's suits, ask for discount on accessories - for example, cufflinks, tie pins or handkerchiefs.

⊛ For stationary, if you're not making your own, get it all from one supplier.

⊛ If you're having your bouquets arranged by a florist and you'd really like flower centerpieces or decorations, get them all done by the same florist.

Some of this might sound like a contradiction on what I've said previously. However, every individual is different. Some brides will be happy to buy their dress and accessories second hand or make their own stationary and yet, some brides would not. The bottom line with everything really is to shop around and find the best deals you can.

Do You Need A Cake?

Cutting the cake has always been a tradition at a wedding, but do you really want or need it? Ranging from around £100 to over £1000, wedding cakes can be incredibly expensive and can potentially take up a big chunk of your budget. If it's something that's not really important to you, consider other options.

There are lots of alternatives to a traditional wedding cake. Cupcakes are a very popular choice for people who still want cake, but not a traditional tiered cake. Doughnuts are also becoming a popular alternative these days. Some other options are cookies, macarons and croquembouche to name a few. Or if you can't decide, you could provide a dessert table, filled with all kinds of desserts and puddings.

While we chose to have cupcakes on our wedding day, we still wanted a cake to cut.

Therefore, we chose to also have a small, iced fruit cake as well. We were lucky enough to have some amazing bakers in our family; my cousin made and decorated all of the cupcakes, and hubby's grandmother made our fruit cake. We also had a plain, iced sheet cake which was cut up and given out to guests.

Sheet cakes can save you a significant amount too. You could have a small decorated cake on show to cut in front of your guests, and then have a large sheet cake which can be cut up for your guests to eat. The point is, no one will see the sheet cake before it's cut up, and therefore requires no decoration, just icing if desired. This makes the cost much less than if you were to have a large cake decorated.

If you don't really have a sweet tooth, you could consider a cheese wedding cake. These are also becoming very popular. They look similar to a traditional tiered cake, but instead of the tiers being made from cake, they are made from different types of cheese! You can even cut it like you would a traditional wedding cake!

Reward Cards

Many credit cards offer rewards. For example, Sainsbury's credit card uses Nectar points, and Tesco credit card has Clubcard points. Try and use these to your advantage by using your credit card to pay for purchases and reap the rewards. If you can, make sure you pay it off at the end of the month when you get your statement to avoid any unnecessary charges.

With American Express credit cards, you can acquire Avios. This can be great if you're planning on honeymooning abroad because your Avios points can be used to get money off flights and hotels. The only disadvantage to American Express is that some stores will not accept it as payment due to high charges they can incur.

Cash back cards can also be a good way to get a little back when you spend. These cards basically work by paying you a percentage of cash back every time you spend on them.

Shop around because different cash back cards offer different rewards.

Disclaimer: This information does not constitute, nor is it intended as financial advice or a recommendation of the mentioned companies. I have no affiliation with them whatsoever. This information is intended as an example only.

Ditch the "Traditions"

Weddings are expensive, we all know that. But you could save so much money by simply forgetting about traditions.

Think about it. Do you really need favours? It's highly likely that your guests will eat whatever goodies are inside and leave the packaging on the table or chuck it in the bottom of their bag and forget about it. Would your guests even notice if you didn't have favours? Probably not. So, consider foregoing them to save yourself some money that could be better spent elsewhere. Alternatively, if you're having a sweet table, provide sweet bags and encourage your guests to help themselves. That way, you're not paying out any extra because you already have the sweets anyway.

This is actually what we did. We were already doing our own sweet table instead of hiring a sweet cart to save money. The sweet jars were arranged on a table in the hallway just outside the banqueting suite. We then bought small paper bags and labels, which we used as favour bags, and doubled up their purpose as place names with each guest's name label being attached to the bag at their place on the table. Inside each bag was a small piece of card with a poem on it explaining that the bag belonged to them and that they could fill it with the sweets of their choice from the sweet table. This worked really well, and our guests also used their bags to take some cake home at the end of the night.

As I mentioned before, think about swapping a traditional cake for an alternative, like a dessert table or cupcakes. Having a cake has always been tradition, but it's not a necessity, especially as you probably won't get a chance to eat any on the night anyway.

Wearing a veil is another old tradition. However, these days, it seems to be more about fashion than anything else. If you want a veil, go for it. But if you don't, there's no point spending more money unnecessarily.

Having a formal sit down meal is usually the done thing on your wedding day, but as I mentioned before, there are alternatives to this. Having a buffet, hog roast or barbecue are just a few options.

To Conclude

Throughout this book we have discussed a variety of different things surrounding your Wedding Budget.

We talked about how you can make more of your income available to save for your wedding. You should also have a clearer idea of how exactly to allocate your budget to the various different cost areas.

Additionally, we talked at length about the numerous ways you can be smart with your budget and reduce costs for specific areas of your wedding.

So, there you have it; my secrets, tips and advice on how to plan your dream wedding under budget without compromising on what you want.

I truly hope that you were able to take something of value away from this book. If all it did was to help one Busy Bride To Be have her dream wedding, then it would be worth it to me.

Has This Book Helped You?

I'd love to hear YOUR story! Let me know how I can help YOU.

It is all very well me writing this book and *hoping* that it will make a difference to someone's life, but, if you have taken something, anything that you learned from this book and it has saved you money, you qualify for my "Busy Bride Budget Award". Head over to www.weddingbudgetaward.com to apply for your Award now!

I'd like to thank you for your time and attention, and I wish you all the best for your wedding planning and your future with your spouse.

28388560R00072

Made in the USA
Columbia, SC
15 October 2018